VITAMIN K$_2$
Keeping Calcium in its Place

*Understanding the importance
of vitamin K$_2$*

Kate Rhéaume-Bleue, ND

Vitamin K₂: Keeping Calcium in its Place

Understanding the importance of vitamin K₂

Mind Publishing

Our focus is education

FOR INFORMATION CONTACT

Mind Publishing Inc.
PO Box 57559,
1031 Brunette Avenue
Coquitlam, BC Canada V3K 1E0
Tel: 604-777-4330 Toll free: 1-877-477-4904
Fax: 1-866-367-5508
Email: info@mindpublishing.com
www.mindpublishing.com

ISBN 978-1-927017-14-2
Printed in Canada

TABLE OF CONTENTS

INTRODUCTION

Are you concerned about bone health, heart health, cancer, or diabetes? Have you been taking calcium or vitamin D? Have you heard conflicting news reports about the safety of calcium supplements? If you answered yes to any of these questions, this booklet is for you. It will introduce you to vitamin K_2, a little-known vitamin with big health benefits.

A new vitamin?

It's not every day you hear of a new vitamin. In fact, it has been decades since anyone "discovered" or identified a novel nutrient with health benefits as profound as vitamin K_2. With so much health information (and dis-information) available today, it's easy to become overwhelmed or skeptical when it comes to the latest, greatest super-nutrient.

But vitamin K_2 is different. This nutrient was once abundant in our diets, protecting us from heart attack, stroke, brittle bones, cancer, and a myriad of other now-all-too-common ailments.

Vitamin K_2 is a nutrient that offers significant health benefits and yet was overlooked for almost 70 years due to a case of mistaken identity. It provides a missing piece to the nutritional puzzle of ailments such as osteoporosis, heart disease, cancer, varicose veins, diabetes, arthritis, and others. In the following pages you will learn what vitamin K_2 is, what it does in the body, how it has all but vanished from our diets, and how we can get it back, as well as how much you need for optimal health, and what to look for in a vitamin K_2 supplement.

My book *Vitamin K_2 and the Calcium Paradox: How a Little-Known Vitamin Could Save Your Life* (Wiley & Sons, 2012) provides comprehensive coverage of everything you need to know about vitamin K_2, including the broad range of benefits possible with vitamin K_2 and a complete list of scientific references supporting the data. You will find some of those references at the back of this booklet.

Kate Rhéaume-Bleue, ND
March 2013

THE CALCIUM CONUNDRUM

For years nutritionists, dieticians, and medical professionals alike have emphasized dietary calcium intake and calcium supplements (along with vitamin D) as the key to strong bones.

Several recent studies have shown that people who take calcium supplements experience significantly more heart attacks and strokes than those who don't. It turns out that a portion of the calcium not taken up by bones ends up lining the arteries, leading to hardening of the arteries, or atherosclerosis (heart disease). However, simply giving up calcium supplements may be shortsighted, since heart disease is the leading killer of both men and women whether or not they take calcium supplements. In other words, calcium can get into the wrong places and cause harm in anyone... but it's not calcium's fault! And calcium is an essential nutrient for healthy teeth and bones.

Looking only at calcium intake, we would never understand why calcium is misdirected from the bones and ends up in the arteries instead. How can we get calcium to go where it's needed? What keeps calcium in its place?

We are not powerless in the face of this calcium conundrum. The body has ways of dealing with this mineral and keeping it where it belongs. North Americans didn't always suffer from heart disease and hip fractures to the extent that we do today. Some developed countries don't have anywhere near the rates of heart attack, stroke or osteoporosis that we have in North America. How is it that the citizens of countries like France and Japan have escaped this calcium conundrum?

As you will see, the diets in those countries, and others, provide high levels of the one nutrient that tells calcium where to go: vitamin K_2.

WHAT IS VITAMIN K$_2$?

Vitamin K$_2$ (menaquinone) is a fat-soluble nutrient that works with vitamin D to guide calcium into bones and teeth and, more importantly, helps keep calcium out of soft tissues like arteries. It also activates special proteins that have powerful cancer-fighting abilities. If you take vitamin D you may see even greater benefits when you supplement with vitamin K$_2$.

How much vitamin K$_2$ are we getting in our daily diet? The short answer is "not enough". Research in 2007 showed that most apparently healthy adults do not have enough dietary vitamin K$_2$ to fully meet their body's requirement for this nutrient. When there isn't enough vitamin K$_2$ to keep calcium in its place all the time, it opens the door to increased risk for heart disease, osteoporosis, cancer, and a number of other serious health conditions. Alternately, having adequate vitamin K_2 intake protects us against all of those health problems and more. But more on that later. Let's take a look at why vitamin K_2 was overlooked for so long.

Vitamin K_1 versus K_2

If you are wondering why you haven't heard about vitamin K_2 until now, it's because it was overlooked for decades and is still often misunderstood. Another form of vitamin K, vitamin K_1 (phylloquinone), stole the spotlight. The body uses vitamin K_1 for blood clotting and it is easily obtained in our diets by eating green leafy vegetables. Vitamin K_1 is so important for coagulation that the body has a special mechanism to reuse vitamin K_1. That means if you only eat green leafy vegetables once in a blue moon, the body can always find and recycle enough K_1 to ensure proper blood clotting. A deficiency of vitamin K_1 is extremely rare. When it does occur, usually as a result of liver disease or some other serious illness, the symptoms of K_1 insufficiency are obvious: bruising and bleeding. The vitamin K_1 recycling mechanism is so efficient that you can afford to take this nutrient for granted; we don't have to worry about our intake of K_1, and there is no need for supplementation. This is not the case with vitamin K_2.

Vitamins K_1 and K_2 were both discovered in the 1930s and at the time researchers assumed they were both blood-clotting vitamins. That assumption caused vitamin K_2 to be ignored for more than two generations.

We eventually learned that vitamin K_2 does not come from green leafy vegetables, does not participate in blood clotting and it is not recycled in the body. Studies show that without vitamin K_2 in our diets on a daily basis, we can become deficient in this nutrient in as little as one week. Furthermore, the symptoms of vitamin K_2 deficiency are not obvious because they are, for the most part, internal. A lack of vitamin K_2, even a marginal deficiency, can permit osteoporosis, heart disease, diabetes, and cancer to quietly creep up on us.

It was long presumed that vitamin K_1 was the more important of these sibling nutrients, since vitamin K_1 is present in much higher amounts in our diet. In fact, although vitamin K_1 is more abundant in foods, we only absorb 5–10% of what we ingest. On the other hand, while vitamin K_2 is less plentiful in the diet, we absorb almost 100% of what we consume. That makes the dietary contribution from vitamins K_1 and K_2 about equal. The difference is that we have a back up mechanism to prevent vitamin K_1 deficiency that doesn't exist for vitamin K_2, so we need to be more mindful of our vitamin K_2 intake.

When we consume the pro-coagulant vitamin K_1 from vegetables it is transported from the intestines to the liver, where it aids the body's coagulation mechanisms. Calcium-controlling vitamin K_2 from foods is also transported to the liver after absorption, but is not destined to stay there. Instead, it is packaged up and sent back out into circulation so it can reach the heart, brain, bones, and other tissues where it facilitates healing. Below is a chart that compares these two nutrients at a glance. Understanding the difference between them will help you ensure you are getting the right kind of vitamin K in your diet and supplements.

Vitamin K_1 vs. vitamin K_2*		
	K_1 (phylloquinone)	K_2 (menaquinone)
Physiological action	Blood clotting	Appropriate calcification
Food sources	Green leafy vegetables	Natto (fermented soybeans), goose liver, certain cheeses, egg yolks and dairy product from grass-fed animals
Can be recycled by the body	Yes (so dietary requirements are minimal)	No (so dietary intake is crucial)
Deficiency	Very rare, leads to bleeding	Common – manifests as osteoporosis, heart disease, cancer, varicose veins, etc.
Ability to build bone and fight heart disease	Slight	Significant

*Adapted from: Rhéaume-Bleue, K. *Vitamin K_2 and the Calcium Paradox: How a Little-Known Vitamin Could Save Your Life.* Wiley & Sons, 2012.

MAJOR HEALTH BENEFITS OF VITAMIN K$_2$

Now you know that vitamin K$_2$ doesn't participate in coagulation. Instead, it ushers calcium into the right places and out of the wrong places. This makes it especially helpful for bone health, heart health and, surprisingly, cancer prevention. We'll examine each of these major benefits individually.

Bone health

While your skeleton seems solid and unchanging, bones are in fact constantly being broken down and rebuilt (a process called remodeling) to maintain strong, healthy bone tissue. If, over time, the breaking down process exceeds the rate of rebuilding, bones lose their density, becoming more porous, brittle and prone to breaking, a condition known as osteoporosis. Up to 50% of women and 30% of men experience fractures due to osteoporosis. You may not realize it, but this is a significant cause of death, since many people die due to complications following a fracture. Many of those who survive bone fractures never again live or walk independently. Osteoporosis prevention is therefore extremely important.

For years the standard non-prescription recommendation for osteoporosis prevention and treatment began and ended with calcium and vitamin D. Calcium and vitamin D absolutely help increase bone density, but not always as much as we'd like. The recommended dose of calcium has gradually increased to 1200, 1500 and even 2000 mg daily. These huge doses of calcium are based on the idea that, if a little is good then more is better. Based on that logic, if we just took enough calcium it would cure osteoporosis. But it doesn't work that way. Merely taking calcium, with or without vitamin D, provides no guarantee that the mineral is getting into our bones and staying there. Keeping calcium in our bones is the job of vitamin K_2.

Vitamin K$_2$ and your bones

Vitamin K$_2$ boosts bone health in a number of ways. Very simply, it activates a protein called osteocalcin that takes dietary calcium and guides it into bones and teeth to improve bone mineral density (BMD).

Studies show vitamins K$_2$ and D$_3$ together increase BMD far better than either nutrient alone. But the bone benefits of vitamin K$_2$ go beyond its effect on bone density. BMD is only one aspect of bone health, although it's the one that gets the most attention. Vitamin K$_2$'s ability to improve bone quality and strength, and reduce fracture risk, is significantly greater than its impact on BMD.

Osteoporosis becomes a greater concern for women after menopause. The natural decline of estrogen can negatively impact bone strength in multiple ways. Vitamin K$_2$ has been shown to fight osteoporosis by counteracting these changes in bone health. In areas where vitamin K$_2$ consumption is high (in certain regions of Japan, for example) osteoporosis is uncommon and women experience far fewer bone fractures. In other words, osteoporosis is not inevitable.

For women, increasing vitamin K$_2$ intake and/or taking a vitamin K$_2$ supplement is extremely important as menopause approaches, to help prevent the onset of bone loss. That being said, many women only learn about vitamin K_2 later in life, when osteopenia (mild or pre-osteoporosis) or even more severe bone loss has already set in. Even then, it's not too late to benefit from vitamin K_2.

How quickly improved bone health occurs after increasing vitamin K_2 intake varies from person to person. The most recent clinical trials show that the maximum benefits for bone and heart health are seen within 2–3 years. That may sound like a long time, but keep in mind that osteoporosis and heart disease don't develop overnight. It took decades of K_2 deficiency for calcium to leech out of bones and build up in arteries. A significant improvement within 2–3 years is worth waiting for.

Heart health

For years the major focus of cardiovascular disease prevention and treatment has revolved around cholesterol. People are encouraged to eat foods with no or low cholesterol, to have their cholesterol levels tested, and to take medications to reduce it, if necessary. Given this cholesterol fixation, it might surprise you to learn that 50% of people who have heart attacks have normal cholesterol levels. How can that be?

It turns out that whether cholesterol is high, low, or normal, what actually clogs arteries is calcium-laden arterial plaque.

Calcium has the potential to accumulate on the inner walls of arteries in a process called atherosclerosis or "hardening of the arteries". This can eventually cause a blockage in one or more of the arteries that provide blood to the heart, resulting in a heart attack. If the blockage happens in the brain, the result is a stroke. The amount of calcium found in arteries is directly proportional to the amount of arterial blockage – and to the risk of suffering a heart attack. While recent studies point the finger at calcium supplements as a factor in heart attack and stroke, the fact is that heart disease is the number one cause of death for people who don't take calcium supplements too. That means we all need to do what we can to keep calcium out of our arteries, and abandoning calcium supplements provides no assurance of clear arteries.

Cleaning up arterial calcium

The body has a number of safeguards to prevent and reverse hardening of the arteries. Of these mechanisms, scientists agree that one is particularly important and powerful. It involves a vitamin-K_2-dependent protein called MGP (matrix gla protein). MGP is produced in soft tissues, such as blood vessels, but it remains inactive until vitamin K_2 arrives to switch it on. Once activated by vitamin K_2, MGP will scour blood vessels of calcium deposits.

Vitamin-K_2-activated MGP removes calcium from areas where calcium is not supposed to be, such as arteries, veins, and other soft tissues. Reversing heart disease may sound incredible, but the body has always had the means to prevent and reverse the build up of arterial plaque; it just needs certain nutrients (notably vitamin K_2) to do it. The scarcity of vitamin K_2 in our modern diets is one of the reasons heart disease – which used to be rare and is still much less common in some countries – has become the leading killer of men and women in North America.

Vitamin K_2 has been shown to reduce arterial calcification and improve blood vessel flexibility. This effect is seen not just in the coronary arteries that feed the heart itself, but also in the aorta, the heart valves, and just about every other blood vessel in the body.

Cancer protection

Vitamin K_2 activates a third protein, "growth arrest sequence-6 protein" or Gas6, which regulates cell growth. This makes K_2 a powerful ally in preventing and defeating cancer. Studies show K_2 encourages cancer cells to die or differentiate into normal, healthy, non-cancerous cell types. For this reason K_2 has important anti-cancer effects throughout the body.

The European Prospective Investigation into Cancer (EPIC) study followed 24,000 men and women over ten years to determine risk factors for cancer. It found that people with the highest intake of vitamin K_2 had a 30% lower rate of cancer, and death from cancer, than people with low K_2 intakes. This was especially true for lung and prostate cancer, the two biggest cancer killers of men. The study found that the greatest dietary source of vitamin K_2 in the European diet was cheese, and that cheese consumption had a significant impact on cancer prevention.

Multiple studies demonstrate the importance of K_2 for different kinds of cancer. Vitamin K_2 has been shown to delay the onset of liver cancer in people with hepatitis and has a positive impact on leukemia. Further studies show K_2 combats cancer in the colon, stomach, brain, breast, nose, throat, and mouth.

OTHER BENEFITS OF VITAMIN K₂

Anti-aging

The most important new theory of aging is called the triage theory. It suggests that when dietary availability of a vitamin or mineral is moderately inadequate, nature will ensure that essential short-term survival body functions are protected, at the expense of long-term needs, such as prevention of aging. In other words, if we are even slightly lacking in nutrient intake we might not notice it today, but we'll pay for it in the future in terms of having more age-related complaints. An optimal daily intake of dietary nutrients, therefore, is one that meets our needs not just for today but for a lifetime.

While the triage theory does not imply that any one vitamin or mineral deficiency is the cause of age-related disease, the theory's authors did test their theory by examining vitamin K. Simply put, short-term inadequacy of K vitamins has been shown to have long-term health consequences. Since we know that vitamin K_1 deficiency is rare due to recycling, that leaves adequate vitamin K_2 intake as the critical factor in preventing such ravages of time as osteoporosis, heart disease, cancer, and even wrinkles.

Brain and neurological health

The brain contains one of the highest concentrations of vitamin K_2 in the body and this nutrient plays several important roles in the health of the brain and nervous system. For example, vitamin K_2 has been shown to prevent brain damage associated with lack of oxygen. If brain cells are deprived of oxygen for any reason, they can be permanently damaged. This can happen in conditions such as strokes and TIAs (transient ischemic attacks or recurrent "mini-strokes"). If oxygen supply to the brain is interrupted during birth, this can lead to cerebral palsy, with lifelong consequences. Fat-soluble-vitamin research states that taking vitamin K_2 during pregnancy could prevent cerebral palsy. Similarly, vitamin K_2 can potentially buffer the damage done to brain cells due to lack of oxygen during a stroke or TIA.

Vitamin K_2 also interferes with the formation of free radicals in the brain, helping to prevent or delay the onset of Alzheimer's disease and other forms of dementia, and age-related brain degeneration.

Dental and oral health

Just under your tooth's enamel (the outermost and visible layer) lies a layer of tissue called dentin. Unlike enamel, dentin has the potential to continue to form throughout life. Dentin also produces MGP, which plays a critical role in maintaining dental health. In fact, although the body doesn't really store much vitamin K_2, it does concentrate vitamin K_2 in the saliva glands, so this important nutrient is delivered directly to the teeth and gums. When vitamin K_2 is abundant, it helps teeth resist the action of bacteria that might otherwise eat holes through the enamel and into the dentin. Vitamin K_2 complements good cavity-fighting oral hygiene. Anecdotally, many people who take vitamin K_2 supplements report a lessening of dental plaque and tartar and improved gum health.

Diabetes

Osteocalcin, the vitamin-K_2-dependent bone-building protein, has been shown to influence insulin sensitivity.

Insulin is a hormone that allows dietary sugar from our blood stream to enter the body's cells to provide energy. Adult onset or type 2 diabetes exists when the pancreas produces insulin but the body's cells don't respond to it efficiently. Consequently sugar continues to circulate in the blood stream longer than it should, which can lead to many serious health problems.

Vitamin K_2 deficiency may be a key reason why people with diabetes are prone to osteoporosis, heart disease, and kidney disease. In clinical trials vitamin K_2 supplementation has been shown to improve insulin resistance, helping the body's cells to fight diabetes.

Wrinkles

Calcium can accumulate microscopically on the elastic tissues in the skin. When this happens, skin becomes less elastic and sags. Vitamin K_2 fights skin aging and the development of wrinkles by protecting the elasticity of skin in the same way it safeguards the elasticity of arteries and veins. No need to apply it topically though, the same K_2 you take to protect your bones and heart will work its magic on your skin from the inside.

Varicose veins

Vitamin K_2 plays an important role in preventing and healing varicose veins. Calcium can accumulate in the walls of veins in a similar fashion to the way it accumulates in arteries. This can slow blood flow, causing the veins to bulge out, eventually becoming distended, hard, and prominently visible through the skin. MGP, the same vitamin-K_2-dependent protein that protects arteries, is involved here. While family history predisposes us to varicose veins, vitamin K_2 intake is a controllable factor that can help minimize unsightly vein appearance and discomfort.

Muscle cramps

Although generally associated with sports injuries, muscle cramping also affects non-athletes. Muscle cramps are common in adults and become increasingly frequent with age. Thirty percent of people over the age of 60, and 50% of people over the age of 80, suffer with occasional or frequent leg muscle spasms. Leg cramps (sometimes called a "charley horse") can last from a few seconds to several hours and may wake sufferers at night.

Vitamin K_2 (in the form of MK-7) has been shown to decrease the frequency and severity of leg cramps. Leg cramps gradually return if vitamin K_2 is discontinued. Magnesium supplementation is also helpful for muscle cramps.

Fertility

Osteocalcin, the same vitamin-K_2-dependent protein that builds bones and teeth, has a significant influence on sperm production. Osteocalcin binds to cells in the testicles that produce testosterone and boost sperm count. Couples planning a family or trying to conceive should ensure both partners are getting optimal amounts of vitamin K_2.

Facial development

During pregnancy vitamin K_2 has a major impact on the healthy development of the facial structures of the fetus. Adequate vitamin K_2 intake helps ensure a wide, healthy facial structure with lots of room for the adult teeth to eventually grow into place. A vitamin K_2 deficiency during pregnancy, on the other hand, causes development of a narrower jaw that can lead to crowded teeth or the need for orthodontics (braces).

WHO BENEFITS FROM VITAMIN K_2?

As you have no doubt realized, the many health benefits of vitamin K_2 make this an essential nutrient for a healthy life. Specifically, vitamin K_2 is as important as folic acid is for pregnant women. In the first trimester the nutrient is critical for the development of primary teeth and healthy facial structure; in the second trimester the formation of adult teeth and the skeleton requires K_2. Despite the importance of K_2 in early pregnancy, studies show that K_2 levels tend to be at their lowest in the third trimester, so expectant mothers should continue to pay attention to their K_2 intake at that time. Experts conclude that adequate K_2 intake during pregnancy may prevent cerebral palsy caused by birth trauma.

Vitamin K_2 intake continues to be crucial during childhood and adolescence, since the rate of bone growth and turnover is highest at that time. Children and teens have especially high requirements for vitamin K_2 to nourish their growing bodies and ensure healthy teeth and bones.

Vitamin K_2 has also been shown to counteract the negative changes in bone density experienced by menopausal women. Both men and women over 50 show serious vitamin K_2 deficiencies, accelerating the rate of bone loss and vascular calcification.

SOURCES OF VITAMIN K_2

Vitamin K_2 from foods

We've talked about where you can't get dietary vitamin K_2 – from green leafy vegetables – so where can you get it?

Dietary vitamin K_2 comes from two main sources: animal fat, such as egg yolks, butter, and dairy products, and certain fermented foods. Animals accumulate vitamin K_2 in their tissues in direct proportion to the K_1 in their diets. Since green plants are the primary source of vitamin K_1, that means meat and dairy products from grass-fed animals are much richer in this nutrient than the products of their grain-fed counterparts. If you have ever seen the deep orange colour of a truly free-range (outdoor) egg yolk you were looking at a vitamin K_2-rich egg. Free-range eggs are 4–5 times higher in K_2 than their conventional counterparts.

Although meat, eggs, and butter (from grass-fed or free-range animals) are good sources of vitamin K_2, these foods can be hard to find. European studies suggest that meat and eggs aren't the predominant source of vitamin K_2 in the Western diet; fermented dairy products are. Certain bacteria produce vitamin K_2, which is why some (but not all) fermented dairy products are rich in vitamin K_2. Gouda and Brie cheeses are especially high in vitamin K_2. A 3 oz portion of Gouda, for example, provides almost one-third of an optimal daily intake of 200 mcg of vitamin K_2. The same amount of Brie provides about 50 mcg, or 25% of the optimal daily intake. Yogurt and kefir, by comparison, have little or no vitamin K_2 since the bacteria that make those foods don't produce vitamin K_2.

But aren't egg yolks, butter, and cheese the very foods we were warned against for years as being sources of "artery-clogging" saturated fat? Yes, and fortunately that outdated and entirely inaccurate notion is no longer recognized in current nutrition research, even though it stubbornly lingers in popular nutrition "myth". In fact the high amounts of artery-clearing vitamin K_2 in these very foods explains the French Paradox, how the French are able to enjoy low rates of heart disease despite high-fat diets. It's not just the red wine: classic creamy French sauces, Brie, and even goose liver pâté are all excellent sources of vitamin K_2.

Vitamin K_2 content of selected foods

Food 3 ½ ounce portion	Micro-gram (μg)	Proportion of vitamin K_2	Food 3 ½ ounce portion	Micro-gram (μg)	Proportion of vitamin K_2
Natto, cooked	1,103.4	(90% MK-7, 10% other MK)	Chicken Leg	8.5	(100% MK-4)
Goose liver pâté	369.0	(100% MK-4)	Ground beef (medium fat)	8.1	(100% MK-4)
Hard cheeses (Dutch Gouda style), raw	76.3	(6% MK-4, 94% other MK)	Chicken liver (braised)	6.7	(100% MK-4)
Soft cheeses (French Brie style)	56.5	(6.5 MK-4, 93.5% other MK)	Hot dog	5.7	(100% MK-4)
Egg yolk, (Netherlands)	32.1	(98% MK-4, 2% other MK)	Bacon	5.6	(100% MK-4)
Goose leg	31.0	(100% MK-4)	Calf's liver (pan-fried)	6.0	(100% MK-4)
Egg yolk (U.S.)	15.5	(100% MK-4)	Sauerkraut	4.8	(100% MK-4)
Butter	15.0	(100% MK-4)	Whole milk	1.0	(100% MK-4)
Chicken liver (raw)	14.1	(100% MK-4)	Salmon (Alaska, Coho, Sockeye, Chum, and King wild (raw))	0.5	(100% MK-4)
Chicken liver (pan-fried)	12.6	(100% MK-4)	Cow's liver (pan-fried)	0.4	(100% MK-4)
Cheddar cheese (U.S.)	10.2	(6% MK-4, 94% other MK)	Egg white	0.4	(100% MK-4)
Meat franks	9.8	(100% MK-4)	Skim milk	0.0	(100% MK-4)
Chicken breast	8.9	(100% MK-4)			

Table from Rhéaume-Bleue, K. *Vitamin K_2 and the Calcium Paradox: How a Little-Known Vitamin Could Save Your Life.* John Wiley & Sons Canada, 2012, p. 66-67.

The Japanese have also been singled out as having great heart health, and their diet is nothing like the French diet. But they do have a unique dietary source of vitamin K_2. Natto, a fermented Japanese soybean food, contains more vitamin K_2 than any other known food. One 40 g serving of natto contains as much as 450 mcg of vitamin K_2. Studies show a statistically significant inverse relationship between natto consumption and hip fracture in Japan. In other words, people who eat vitamin K_2-rich natto experience fewer hip fractures than those who don't. The form of vitamin K_2 found in natto has been shown to be especially helpful for bone and heart health. Unfortunately this unusual superfood is hard to find in North America and most Western palates are put off by natto's odour and flavour.

Other fermented soy foods such as miso and tempeh, or unfermented soy products such as tofu and soymilk, do not contain any vitamin K_2. If you can't find natto at a local Asian market – nor learn to appreciate its unique taste and texture – then look for natto-derived vitamin K_2 supplements. These will indicate "from natto" as the source, or have the designation "menaquinone-7" (or MK-7) somewhere on the label.

Vitamin K_2 from supplements

Since meat and dairy from grass-fed animals are not readily available, natto can be hard to love, and cheese is a challenge when watching your weight, vitamin K_2 supplements may be the best, most consistent, convenient source of life-saving vitamin K_2. There are two different types of K_2 supplements on store shelves. Understanding the big difference between them is key to getting the results you seek.

Menaquinone-7 (MK-7) supplements

As mentioned above, MK-7 is a form of vitamin K_2 derived from the Japanese fermented soybean food called natto. This form of vitamin K_2 offers several advantages over other forms. MK-7 has a long half-life in the body, meaning it circulates in the blood for a day or two, which means that a convenient, single daily dose will meet your menaquinone needs. Because this form of vitamin K_2 stays in the blood longer, MK-7 can be effective in relatively small amounts. About 200 mcg of MK-7 per day is required to meet the body's need for K_2 and to activate all K_2-dependent proteins. The majority of clinical trials on adults were conducted using approximately 200 mcg of MK-7, although people who eat natto daily get at least twice that amount from their diet.

For anyone concerned about the potentially harmful effects of some soy products, fermented soy poses no such problems, and vitamin K_2 supplements from soy do not contain any harmful soy compounds. Unless someone has a true anaphylactic allergy to soy, which is rare, MK-7 is the best choice among the vitamin K_2 supplements.

Menaquinone-4 (MK-4) supplements

The other type of vitamin K_2 supplement that persists on store shelves is menaquinone-4. MK-4 is a synthetic form of vitamin K_2 that was one of the early vitamin K_2 supplement forms. Although many scientific studies have used MK-4, it has several limitations, especially in terms of the required dose. The therapeutic dose of MK-4 used in most research is 45 mg (45,000 mcg). This dose is permitted in the USA but far exceeds the Health Canada limit of 120 mcg per dose. Imagine if someone owed you $45,000 but only paid you $120? MK-4 products are simply ineffective at such a low dose.

Proponents of MK-4 point out that it is the type of vitamin K_2 that occurs naturally in animal-derived foods such as egg yolks and butter. While that is true, the MK-4 found in supplements is not extracted from these natural sources, it is synthesized in a laboratory. MK-7, on the other hand, is extracted from food and identical to what is found in natto. Just as natural vitamin D_3 has gradually replaced synthetic vitamin D_2 in most supplements, natural MK-7 will soon replace synthetic MK-4 on store shelves.

The following chart summarizes some of the key differences between MK-4 and MK-7.

	Menaquinone-4 (MK-4)	Menaquinone-7 (MK-7)
Source	Synthetic	Natural, food-based
Recommended dosage	45 mg (45,000 mcg)	200–400 mcg
Dosing frequency	Divided dose, three times daily	Once daily
Half life in body	A few hours, hence the need for frequent dosing	A few days, so a single daily dose is fine

If the supplement you are considering just lists "vitamin K" and doesn't indicate whether it contains vitamin K_1 or vitamin K_2, MK-4 or MK-7, don't buy it. There's no way to tell what you are buying and whether it will deliver all the benefits of vitamin K_2. Additionally, there's no need to spend money on supplements that contain vitamin K_1 since this nutrient easily obtained from the diet, the body recycles it, and deficiencies are extremely rare.

DOSAGE, SAFETY, AND DRUG INTERACTIONS

Vitamin K_2 is very safe for adults and children, with no known toxic effects, unlike some other fat-soluble vitamins. A popular misconception is that high vitamin K_1 or vitamin K_2 intake will promote blood clots. Vitamin K supplements have no clotting effect, since coagulation proteins are already fully activated by vitamin K_1 in people who are not on blood-thinning medications.

On the topic of medications, vitamin K_2 supplements have no drug interactions, except in the case of warfarin (Coumadin). Because this type of blood thinner works by limiting the body's vitamin K metabolism, vitamin K supplements may interfere with the drug's efficacy. That being said, studies show that up to 50 mcg of vitamin K_2

(MK-7) can safely be taken with warfarin and may help the medication work more predictably and with fewer side effects. If you are taking a warfarin-type blood thinner, speak to a health care practitioner prior to supplementing with vitamin K_2.

Other so-called "blood-thinning" medications such as aspirin, anti-platelet aggregators (e.g., Plavix), non-warfarin-type blood thinners (e.g., Pradaxa), cardiac medications, and other drugs do not interact with vitamin K_2.

As mentioned previously, current research shows the optimal daily dose of vitamin K_2 (MK-7) is around 200 mcg. Since most MK-7 supplements contain 100–120 mcg per capsule or softgel, two per day will meet most needs. It's worth noting that frequent natto eaters safely get a lot more than 200 mcg of MK-7 in their diet. Since this is a fat-soluble vitamin it's best taken with food for maximum absorption.

CALCIUM AND MAGNESIUM

Although we've touched on calcium several times already, you might still be wondering if you should be taking calcium or not. And, if you should be taking calcium, then how much? It's important to remember that in some countries, like Japan, calcium intake is typically only 400–500 mg per day. Bone density is similar to North America (with our much higher calcium intake), but the Japanese have far fewer hip fractures. Again, it's not about the calcium, but what keeps calcium in its place, as well as aspects of bone strength and quality other than just bone mineral density.

That being said, if you have been diagnosed with osteopenia or osteoporosis, studies show a calcium supplement, along with vitamins D and K_2, will help lower fracture risk. Conventional calcium recommendations – based on the idea that if a little is good then more is better – fall in the range of 1200–1800 mg daily. Instead of those high doses, you could take a cue from the bone-healthy Japanese and limit calcium supplements to around 500 mg daily while making sure you get enough vitamin K_2. Since most people also obtain calcium from their diets, supplementing with 500 mg daily should be sufficient.

We've discussed calcium, but have barely mentioned its partner, magnesium. Calcium and magnesium work hand in hand, and balance one another. Magnesium deficiency is common, and supplementing only with calcium can exacerbate a magnesium deficiency. This is certainly an important criticism of the calcium/heart health studies: none of them took magnesium intake into consideration. Magnesium has at least one very important cardiovascular health benefit: the ability to lower blood pressure. Maintaining healthy blood pressure is a critical factor in minimizing heart attack risk. If you are taking calcium you should also supplement with magnesium – in equal amounts, or at least one part magnesium for every two parts calcium (a 2:1 ratio of calcium to magnesium). For example, if you are taking 600 mg of calcium, then take 300–600 mg of magnesium. Even if you are not taking calcium, consider taking a magnesium supplement.

SUMMARY

Vitamin K_2 is the missing piece to the puzzle of many common ailments. Deficiency of this critically important nutrient has become widespread due to the "industrialization" of our food supply in ways that have reduced our K_2 intake. The result is skyrocketing rates of heart disease, osteoporosis, cancer, diabetes, and other ailments that are often accepted as "just a part of aging".

Moving away from factory farming and getting back to old-fashioned ways of producing food would help restore our vitamin K_2 status but that will take time. Meanwhile, we can consume certain foods (like Gouda, Brie, and natto) to boost our vitamin K_2 consumption, and take advantage of supplements to ensure our daily K_2 intake is adequate.

Readers interested in learning more about vitamin K$_2$ or who would like the complete list of scientific references can check out my book *Vitamin K$_2$ and the Calcium Paradox: How a Little-Known Vitamin Could Save Your Life* (Wiley & Sons, 2012).

REFERENCES

Badmaev V. Therapeutic Activity and Safety of Vitamin K 2-7 in Muscle Cramps. *The Indian Practitioner.* May 2010;vol 63(5):287-291.

Fujita T, Fukase M. Comparison of osteoporosis and calcium intake between Japan and the United States. *Proc Soc Exp Biol Med.* 1992 Jun;200(2):149-52.

Howe AM, Webster WS. Vitamin K – its essential role in craniofacial development.
A review of the literature regarding vitamin K and craniofacial development. *Aust Dent J.* 1994 Apr;39(2):88-92.

Knapen MH, Jie KS, Hamulyák K, et al. Vitamin K-induced changes in markers for osteoblast activity and urinary calcium loss. *Calcif Tissue Int.* 1993 Aug;53(2):81-85.

Lamson DW, Plaza SM. The anticancer effects of vitamin K. *Alt Med Rev.* 2003; 8:303-318.

Li K, Kaaks R, Linseisen J, et al. Associations of dietary calcium intake and calcium supplementation with myocardial infarction and stroke risk and overall cardiovascular mortality in the Heidelberg cohort of the European Prospective Investigation into Cancer and Nutrition study (EPIC-Heidelberg) *Heart.* 2012;98:920-925.

Masterjohn C. On the trail of the elusive X factor. *Wise Traditions*. 2007;(8)1:14-32.

McCann JM, Ames BN. Vitamin K, an example of triage theory: is micronutrient inadequacy linked to diseases of aging? *Am J Clin Nutr*. 2009;90:889-907.

Nimptsch K, Rohrmann S, Kaaks R, et al. Dietary vitamin K intake in relation to cancer incidence and mortality:results from the Heidelberg cohort of the European Prospective Investigation into Cancer and Nutrition (EPIC-Heidelberg). *Am J Clin Nutr*. 2010;91:1348-58.

van Summeren M, Braam L, Noirt F, et al. Pronounced elevation of undercarboxylated osteocalcin in healthy children. *Pediatr Res*. 2007 Mar;61(3):366-70.

Vermeer C. Vitamin K: the effect on health beyond coagulation – an overview. *Food & Nutrition Research*. 2012;56:5329-34.

Yamaguchi M, Uchiyama S, Tsukamoto Y. Inhibitory effect of menaquinone-7 (vitamin K_2) on the bone-resorbing factors-induced bone resorption in elderly female rat femoral tissues in vitro. *Mol Cell Biochem*. 2003 Mar;245(1-2):115-20.